COURAGE
TO
STAND
TALL

BY **DONNEY SALAZAR**

COURAGE TO STAND TALL

Published by
DFS Marketing LLC
www.donneysalazar.com

Copyright © 2019 by Donney Salazar

All rights reserved. Except as permitted under the U.S. Copyright Act of 1976, no part of this publication may be reproduced, distributed, or transmitted in any form or by any means, or stored in a database or retrieval system, without the prior written permission of the publisher.

Printed in the United States of America

First Printing: November 2019

Book cover and interior layout design by Vickie Swisher, Studio 20|20

ISBN 978-0-578-59630-3 (softcover)

TO **MY KIDS**

*I was once given advice from my own father
when I was a young boy.
I now give that advice to you.*

*"You can do anything
as long as you put your mind to it.
There ain't nothing to it, but to do it."*

CONTENTS

Testimonials VII

Foreword XI

Acknowledgements XV

Preface: The Elephant Rope XVII

Chapter 1: The Courage to Walk Away 1

Chapter 2: The Courage to Be Different 11

Chapter 3: The Courage to Fight 19

Chapter 4: The Courage to Let Others In 27

Chapter 5: The Courage to Jump 37

Chapter 6: The Courage to Speak 43

Chapter 7: The Courage to Change 53

Chapter 8: The Courage to Trust 67

Chapter 9: The Courage to Believe 79

Chapter 10: The Courage to Stay 89

Chapter 11: The Courage to Run...................... 95

Chapter 12: The Courage to Stand Tall 107

The Elephant Rope 113

Book Donney to Speak 117

About The Author 119

TESTIMONIALS

"Donney is a very humble, successful individual and good at what he does. He cares about people and genuinely wants them to succeed and can help you do the same!"

~ ADAM DAVIS, DIRECTOR, WFG

"Donney has real life experience that easily relates to everyone. From his childhood, to his faith, his family, and business experience (both in corporate America and in running his own business). Donney has great stories and insights into helping you shift from where you are to where you want to be. Everyone loved Donney and we will definitely have him back! "

~ RICK POULSON, WFG

"Donney's passion makes what he teaches important to everyone. His charisma makes his session riveting, and you just want him to keep talking after his time is up, and how many people can you say that for? Wonderful man, wonderful experience!"

~ CLINT LAWTON, WFG

"After going through some challenging times, and some staff changes in my physical therapy clinic, we were in need of improving the motivation and culture in my staff. We were not as productive as we needed to be, and really weren't working as a team.

I invited Donney to come do a presentation to my staff on his Courage to Shift principles, and it was just what we needed. The experiences he shared and the examples of how to shift our mindset to change our situation was helpful for all of us.

We were able to make changes in our procedures to be more efficient and be more in line with our goals, but I think my employees were also affected to make changes in their own lives.

Overall a great experience and I will definitely have him back to talk to new employees and staff in the future to help them to also shift their work and personal lives."

~ DAVID BUTLER, UTAH PHYSICAL THERAPY

"On behalf of Provo Canyon School, we would like to express our gratitude for Donney's presentation "Courage to Stand Tall." Given that our adolescent population has been exposed to many of the social problems shared in his presentation, our students were able to connect and apply Donney's message to their current life situation. Donney's charisma, personal anecdotes and life experiences encouraged our students to make the necessary changes to better their future and have the courage to be different. Our campus is already experiencing change and positivity thanks to his message."

~ ANA CHAVARRI, TRS CTRS, RECREATIONAL THERAPIST, PROVO CANYON SCHOOL

FOREWORD

I love stories.

Truthfully, people love stories. Stories inspire, stories motivate—stories evoke emotion in people that causes them to respond, to take action, and to adopt your ideas. Robert McKee put it well when he said; "Storytelling is the most powerful way to put ideas into the world today."

Stories are life's currency. We are genetically programmed to learn through stories. It's who we are. It's how we function. Storytelling was the first form of communication historically and is the first form of communication that we encounter as children. As human beings we crave stories. We love to hear stories and we love to share stories. We learn and retain stories before we can read. Our minds intuitively understand story structure and process the message, information and detail contained therein. But stories are more than that. Stories are our universal storehouse of knowledge, beliefs, values, attitudes, passions, dreams, imagination, and vision.

We are constantly exchanging stories, but those who learn to tell stories well have a unique ability to teach, to persuade, to motivate, and to move people.

Most of the work I do today revolves around stories and storytelling. As the author of *The Power of Storytelling*, I speak to audiences and coach people on how they can use their stories to make a bigger impact. And as the host of The Relevant Leadership Podcast, I interview fascinating people to hear their stories and share them with the world.

Every so often you come across a story that is just downright inspiring, riveting, and that is what Donney Salazar's *Courage to Stand Tall* is to the reader. Donney endured an incredibly hard childhood, that by all accounts could have easily broken him. But he made choice after choice to change and we all know change is difficult.

Donny stopped a destructive and harmful cycle by having the courage to be different, to Stand Tall. Donney found his voice. He found his courage. He did what so many are incapable of doing – he saw what was inherently wrong with his situation, where his life could lead and found the courage deep within himself to choose something different.

Joseph Campbell said, "If you are going to have a story, have a big story, or none at all."

Donney has a big story! It's inspiring. It's emotional. And it is insightful.

I highly recommend this book because Donney's story and insights will inspire positive change in your life! My hope is that we all find **THE COURAGE TO STAND TALL**.

TY BENNETT
AUTHOR OF "THE POWER OF STORYTELLING"

ACKNOWLEDGEMENTS

This book has been a lifetime in the making. With the personal experiences I have overcome and the influences that have given me the courage to stand tall, it would only seem right to acknowledge those who have given me this opportunity to share it with you.

To my parents,—thank you for bringing me into this world and for the good and bad influences you were and are in my life. To my older brother,—for pushing me in a different direction without even knowing it.

To the many positive influences, which include, but not limited to: "Papa Bear" my PAL Football coach, and my high school coaches that saw potential in a 5'2" little punk kid. To the Roberts, Rios, and Nelson families—who all at different times, took me in and showed me the true meaning of family, courageous leadership, and selflessness.

To the many friends and family members who helped in the editing of this book, I could not have done this without any one of you.

To my beautiful and supportive wife, Heather Salazar—for continuously pushing and loving me through the process of writing this book—and throughout our journey in this magnificent life. To our amazing ten children—remember you can accomplish anything, as long as you involve Heavenly Father and put your mind to it.

PREFACE
THE ELEPHANT ROPE

"As a man was passing the elephants, he suddenly stopped, confused by the fact that these huge creatures were being held by only a small rope tied to their front leg. No chains, no cages. It was obvious that the elephants could, at anytime, break away from their bonds. But

for some reason, they did not. He saw a trainer nearby and asked why these animals just stood there and made no attempt to get away.

"Well," the trainer said, "When they are very young and much smaller, we use the same size rope to tie them. And at that age, it's enough to hold them. As they grow up, they are conditioned to believe they cannot break away. They believe the rope can still hold them, so they never try to break free."

The man was amazed. These animals could at any time break free from their bonds. But because they believed they couldn't, they were stuck right where they were. Like the elephants, how many of us go through life hanging onto a belief that we cannot do something, simply because we failed at it once before? Failure is part of learning; we should never give up the struggle in life." (6.-The-Elephant-Rope.pdf)

From personal experience, I have found that we tend to be conditioned to think, respond, and feel according to the circumstances we were born in and the behaviors we saw modeled as we grew up. We have no control in what our family life (or lack thereof) will be when we are born—whether horrible or ideal.

Just like the powerful elephant, we are conditioned. When we are young, a figurative rope (our circumstances) is tied to our leg. When we are young, we do not have the power to break that rope because we are dependent upon our parents to provide. As we get older, we grow stronger and more independent. Then suddenly—we have the power and strength to snap that small rope that binds us.

I wrote *Courage to Stand Tall* to show that you can break the minuscule rope of your life's circumstances. You can have a life that you never thought possible by simply finding the courage to stand tall. It doesn't matter what you were born into, or the circumstances that you live in. You have strength that you may have never felt before, and didn't even know was there.

CHAPTER 1

THE COURAGE
TO WALK..........AWAY

> *"It takes great* **COURAGE** *to stand and fight for something. But sometimes it can take even more courage to walk away and leave things behind."*

I often see people who are stuck: Stuck in relationships that keep them from progressing, Stuck in a job that sucks the life out of them, Stuck in a family lifestyle that is leading them in the wrong direction.

Why is it so hard to walk away? Why does it take so much courage to leave?

There could be any number of answers to those questions. For many of us, it is because we have found ourselves in a destructive cycle that we continue to perpetuate.

At the first glance of my childhood, you would see a room decorated with Disney characters and Curious George decor. You would think I had it good. As you looked a little closer, you would realize that wasn't the case.

As a kid, there were times I felt like we lived in a prison. My father was abusive to us kids—but most especially, he abused my mother. We lived in constant fear, unsure of what type of person we would get when the front door opened to announce my father's return home.

One night, my dad came home from work drunk—which wasn't abnormal by any stretch of the imagination. We sat down to dinner with some serious tension in the air. When my dad was drunk, it was like walking through a minefield; everyone was careful not to set him off. We made it through dinner without incident, and were looking forward to the pie my mom had made for dessert.

Rewind for a minute, earlier in the day I had seen the pie in the fridge and couldn't resist dipping my finger in for a taste. When my mom brought out the pie for dessert, you could clearly see the spot I had dipped my finger into.

My dad flipped out! He repeatedly asked who had done it? With every passing second, rage grew. We all sat there terrified and completely silent.

"Who did this?"

I was hoping one of my siblings would take the blame, but no such luck. I finally, timidly, confessed. His anger boiled out, with no thought of the scared little 4-year-old's feelings.

"You like pie?" He said.

"Yes," I said.

He picked up the pie, shoved it in my face and said, "You can have the whole thing to yourself."

This was the first sign to me that we did not have a normal family.

Despite the abuse, most nights I would eagerly wait for my dad to come home. When he arrived, the excited feelings would fade. He would almost instantly start fighting with my mom.

One of the many fights that stands out in my mind is still a dramatic and vivid memory of the constant trouble my father would start. He had come home from work and hadn't liked the way my mom had answered his question. So my father got mad! He began yelling and calling her names, while he chased her up the stairs. Once they reached their room, he picked her up and threw her on the bed, followed by picking up the mattress, and throwing it on top of her.

My mother managed to get away and charged back down the stairs, but my father was right behind her. He caught her in the kitchen, tackled her to the ground, and started slugging her in the face. I ran to help my mom by jumping on his back. I remember punching my dad while yelling for him to stop. He grabbed me and threw me.

That was when my brother stepped in. He was often put in the position of protecting our mother. This was not the first and only time it happened. It was a common occurrence for my father to come home and beat my mom.

One night, it was so bad that she ended up in the hospital with a broken arm, a concussion, and a badly bruised face. I remember my grandmother talking with my mom in the hospital about how she needed to leave my dad. My grandmother was afraid my dad would end up killing my mom one day. My mom knew this, but she was overwhelmed with the fear that he would follow her anyway.

My mom finally got tired of the abuse and worked up the courage to leave. One night she came into my room, woke me up and said, "Be quiet. We are going on a trip, and we can't wake Daddy. Put your shoes and coat on, and follow me."

We walked out of my room and down the stairs to where I saw my brother and sister waiting by the door that led to the garage. We hurried out the door and into the garage where my mom's little black Chevy Camaro was waiting, packed with as much stuff as it could hold. She pulled out of the garage and we were off. My brother asked where we were going and she said California.

My mom spent 14 years being married to my dad and going through the abuse—14 years.

When learning my mother's story, society would likely ask, "So why didn't she leave earlier?" It's a common question that most people ask when they hear stories like mine of domestic violence and abuse. Why don't battered women leave their abusers?

I have done a lot of studying trying to find an answer to this question, and in my research, I found something worth mentioning. According to Michael Down, Director of the Battered Women's Justice Center at Pace University School of Law, asking this question suggests that battered women can control the violence. It also suggests, in a subtle way, that women are to blame when they are unable to leave abusive partners. Victims cannot control the violence that stems from another—no one can. Those responsible for the abusive behavior are the abusers themselves—no one else.

I have discovered that there are several reasons why women stay, and the reasons are usually very compelling. I have also found that there are a number of women who actually do walk away. Usually they accomplish this through the assistance and support of friends, family, and the legal and medical community. Because of the secretive nature of addiction and abuse, there are many who remain in abusive situations in a perpetuated cycle of silence.

For those who do choose to stay, the reasons vary. There are two reasons that tend to show up the most.

The first reason women choose to stay in an abusive relationship is because of **fear**: Fear of the unknown, fear of the future, fear of being on their own, fear of running, even fear of death. Sometimes leaving the abuse, and being alone and on their own, will be more frightening for the victim than remaining in the relationship. Also, quite often, the abuser threatens the victim and the children with physical harm if they try to leave. Statistics show that women who leave their batterers are at a 75% greater risk of being killed by the batterer than those who stay.

The second reason women choose to stay in an abusive relationship is because of **children**. Being a single parent may be a terrifying experience for a battered woman. The responsibility of raising children alone can be too much to bear—even if the spouse or boyfriend has never assisted in the caretaking needs of the children. In addition to this, the abuser will often use the children as a pawn against the victim by threatening to take them away if the woman attempts to leave.

For my mother, I am sure that both of these reasons were a factor. I heard the threats made by my father, and I even saw the fear in my mother's eyes. I am sure she wondered how she was going to take care of us kids, and if we were going to be safe tomorrow. Somehow, my mother was still able to find the courage she needed to walk away.

Although I was only four when my mom left my dad, she taught me a great lesson. She taught me that sometimes the right thing to do is to walk away—even if you are afraid.

There will come times in your life where you will also have to make a choice. Your choice will be whether you are going to stay in a destructive cycle, or choose to walk away and create a different path. Fear may be keeping you stuck, but there is great courage in walking a new path. What destructive cycles are you staying in? I challenge you to really think about this, and find the courage to walk away and choose something better.

(http://www.domesticabuseshelter.org/infodomesticviolence.htm#why)

"Sometimes in life, in order to win, we have to have the **COURAGE** *to stand up and walk away."*

~ **TIFFANY FLETCHER**

CHAPTER 2

THE COURAGE
TO BE DIFFERENT

> *"It takes* **COURAGE** *to be different.*
> *It takes courage to not compromise.*
> *People will try to make you feel weak*
> *because you don't go with the majority.*
> *The truth is you're not weak,*
> *you're strong."*

In order to have the courage to walk away, or the courage to fight, you have to be willing to be different. You can't follow the crowd. But what if the crowd is your family? What if it is your family that is making fun of you and causing you pain? And what if those closest to you are the ones who are leading you in the wrong direction? Would you still have the courage to be different?

The men in my life who were my influences—my leaders—set all kinds of examples for me. Included in those examples was how they viewed women. To them, women were objects to fulfill their needs and desires.

As a five-year-old kid, I witnessed a lot of sexual activity in my home. For example, one night there was a party at our house. There was a lot of people and a lot of drinking—especially my brother's friends. My uncle and his girlfriend were also some of the people at the party, and they both had a lot to drink that night.

The party went into the early morning. Everyone was still there by the time I was getting up for the day. There were people all over the house, passed out and asleep. My uncle's girlfriend was in our living room, while my uncle was in the family room asleep on a chair.

My brother's friends were still up and rowdy. They saw me and asked if I thought that girls were pretty. I was five and naïve to a lot of what was going on around me—but very observant to my surroundings. I said yes, and they started laughing.

They walked over to my uncle's girlfriend and pulled off her clothes. She was very drunk and had passed out, so she did not really respond to what was happening to her. One of the guys got on top of her and did his business—and then another guy. After they were done, they saw me standing there and told me to come over. I said no.

My brother's friends got a little more aggressive with me, so I obeyed and went over to my uncle's girlfriend. They told me to play with her breasts. I said no—but they forced me to.

I was very scared after they left. I took the girl's bra and hid it behind the couch. A couple of hours later, she woke up and was very upset. I am not sure if she knew what had happened to her, and I was too scared to say anything. I remember she was crying. I felt sad and embarrassed for her, and for myself.

A few months later, one of the guys that was involved in the act was in jail, and my uncle went to see him. He told my uncle about what had happened. My uncle then came home and told my mom and one of my brother's friends.

The crazy thing is, no one got angry at the guys. Instead—they teased me about it. Because I was scared to tell anyone, they called me a sissy and a faggot. But that is what they did quite often—tease me about stuff like that.

Even when what they had done had came to light, they showed zero remorse or concern for the girl. And sadly, my mom went right along with them.

I often feel that the reason my mom did not stand up for me was because she had major self-esteem issues. She didn't want to be seen as weak—even if her little boy suffered from what he witnessed. Because I felt insecure about sharing my feelings about the scary things that happened to me, I felt remorse and sadness. I wasn't weak for feeling these emotions—I was five. I was being taught that women were worth*less*.

From the time my mom left my dad, until I was fifteen, I was constantly being exposed to sexually explicit material that degraded women. If I said that I didn't like what I was seeing, or that I was uncomfortable, I would be teased or called names.

One night, my stepfather was extremely high on drugs, while everyone else slept. He was sitting in a recliner when I got up to go to the bathroom, and when he saw me, he called me over. He told me that he wanted me to watch television with him. I told him I wanted to go to bed, but he refused my pleas and forcefully said, "No, you are going to watch this show with me."

With the fear of being yelled at, getting in trouble, or being teased, I stayed. The show that he wanted me to watch was a pornographic movie of women and men having sex. I told him I did not want to watch it. Because of my response, he said that I was a fag and laughed at me. Stuff like this happened a lot with him. He seemed to be targeting me all the time, calling me names and making fun of me if I didn't participate in the behavior he wanted me to.

With all the women in my life being regularly beaten and seen as sexual objects, how does courage to be different apply? In a house of drug addicts, sexual predators, and abuse, I had to find the courage to be different. I knew the actions of the men in my life were wrong, and no matter what the consequences, I had to choose to stand up and be different than them—to treat women with love and respect.

Learning how to treat women with love and respect came as I watched my mother crying after she had been beaten. My heart was softened towards her, and I felt her pain and sadness. I knew then that I never wanted to make a woman feel that kind of pain and sadness. I learned how to treat women by watching the examples around me and deciding that I was going to be different—to show love and respect where they showed hatred, violence, and selfishness. I also learned how to treat women by listening to the lyrics of the love songs that would be constantly playing, as it was the Cholo culture. I found that if I treated women the way the words described, they would feel valued and special.

CHAPTER 2: THE COURAGE TO BE DIFFERENT

"It takes courage to be different, it takes courage to not compromise. People will try to make you feel weak because you don't go with the majority. The truth is you're not weak you are strong."

The courage to be different comes from being willing to see that there is a different way and having the courage to allow the right people in to help show you that way. I may have witnessed men in my life treating women wrong, but I also developed relationships with men who treated women right—and as equals. I found men who put the women in their lives first—where they should be. Because of these positive influences, my wife and eight daughters are treated like a queen and princesses.

Because I had the courage to be different, and to see that women deserved to be treated with love and respect, I broke an abusive cycle in my life, and I changed the course of my future family. My two boys are continually being taught that the women in their lives are to be put above themselves. In addition to this, my daughters are able to see how a woman should be treated when they decide to date or get married. A destructive and harmful cycle ended with me because I had the courage to be different.

What cycles are you stuck in? Are you trying to fit in when you are meant to stand out? How would your life change if you had the courage to be different. Start thinking outside of the box. Be okay with who you are. Stop following the crowd. Most importantly, have the courage to be different.

"People may hate you for being different
and not living by society's standards.
But deep down, they wish they had the
COURAGE *to do the same."*

~ LIVELIFEHAPPY.COM

CHAPTER 3

THE COURAGE
TO FIGHT

> *"There are all kinds of* **COURAGE**.
> *It takes a great deal of bravery to stand up to our enemies, but just as much to stand up to our friends."*
>
> ~ ALBUS DUMBLEDORE

There are many reasons why we would need the courage to walk away, like my mother did in our abusive situation. But sometimes in life, we also have to find the courage to stand up and fight. That is equally important. And even if we don't win the fight, we win by simply having the courage to fight for what we believe in. It's not about winning or losing, it's about taking up the charge to join the battle.

Have you ever watched something happen that you knew was wrong, where you said to yourself, "I should say something, or I should do something!"

Often times, we allow our fears of what people might think of us stop us from fighting for what is right. We tend to hesitate when everyone is watching. But building up the courage to fight for something, or someone, does come. We just need to find our why. I learned at an early age that the courage to fight was in me, and was available to help me at the very moment I understood my why.

Although my mother had escaped the beatings from my dad, she did not take the time needed to fully recover. She, unfortunately, quickly moved into another abusive relationship with my stepfather.

My stepfather is a lot younger than my mom, which I believe made her feel young. However, with him being so young—he was 18 when they were married—he still wanted to be free and not feel tied down. So he constantly cheated on her. The parties never stopped, and everyone would get drunk at them.

One night, my mom and stepfather were drinking and doing drugs, and they got into a fight. My stepfather left my mom, and she went crazy! She chased him down the street with a knife, with me running after her. She saw my brother driving down the street and quickly jumped into the passenger's seat, while I jumped into the car's back seat. My mom then put the knife to her throat and said she was going to kill herself.

Both my brother and I were trying to get the knife from my mom. All our hands were on the knife—pulling and pushing. My brother's hands slipped, and the point of the knife hit me in the chest. I was bleeding. It was a small cut about half an inch deep. I got out of the car—scared. I ran into the house where I saw my uncle and showed him the cut. He said "You are fine! Stop being a baby!"

But I wasn't fine! I had just been stabbed by a knife that my mom was holding to her own throat, threatening to take her own life—I was scared. To this day I still have the scar.

Nights like this seemed to happen more and more. When my stepfather was high on drugs, he would become violent with my mom. I was tired of seeing my mom abused.

So one day, I went to the kitchen and picked out a knife. I told myself that if my stepfather ever hit her again, I was going to stab him.

That day came faster than I had hoped—just a couple days later, when my stepfather was all drugged up. I came home from school and walked into the house to yelling and screaming. He had my mom pinned on the couch, and was violently punching her face. I told him to get off of her, and then I jumped on him to get him to stop, but he pushed me away. I ran to the kitchen, grabbed my chosen knife, and returned to the front room.

"If you don't get off my mom, I will kill you!" I yelled.

He looked at me and started towards me. I got scared. I wasn't prepared for him to come at me. I ran outside and hid the knife under a bush.

This was the first time I found the courage to fight my stepfather. That courage bubbled up from deep within me when I saw that there was a need for it. Someone had to fight for my mother, and I knew it had to be me.

Vanessa Baird writes:
"Who doesn't love a tale of courage?

They pop up in all cultures, traditions and eras. From shepherd-boy David facing giant Goliath, to Gilgamesh defeating the monster Humbaba, to Harry Potter and friends confronting deadly Lord Voldemort.

There's something exhilarating about individuals, pitted against the odds, rising above fear and narrow concerns about self-preservation.

And when real life provides examples of valour, our faith in human nature, in the possibility of virtue, is enhanced."

Richard Avramenko, who teaches political science at the University of Wisconsin, states:

"...courage is the primary means by which humans raise themselves out of their individualistic, isolated and materialistic existence.

Courage...is the willingness to risk life and limb for the sake of something. In other words, courage reveals what we care about... It reveals that which inspires us to overcome ourselves. And it is the self-overcoming character of courage that makes it so poignant. When we are witness to real acts of courage, we know immediately what matters most fundamentally to the courageous actor—and it is not herself, not her own physical well-being."

Finding the courage to fight my stepfather took everything in me. But I knew my why. I was 8-years-old, and for me, my mom was everything. Watching somebody hurt her was painful to watch. I knew I had to stand up and do something. I had to find the courage to fight. This experience with my stepfather, although hard, taught me that I have the ability to protect others—as long as I don't let my fears control me.

As I grew older, I continued to nurture that courage to fight. In my junior year of high school, I was recruited to wrestle by the wrestling coach. He helped me hone my skills and find confidence in my abilities.

I didn't know what to expect as I attended that first practice, but after the warm-ups, the coach pulled me aside. He told me that he wanted me to work on just one thing—takedown. Takedown is when you move in on your opponent, wrap his leg or legs to get him off-balance, and try taking the opponent down. My coach told me he wanted me to master this tactic.

I worked day and night on the takedown. I worked on my speed. And I worked on the power of shooting in on an opponent. To increase my power, I worked on big guys that weighed much more than me. I felt that if I could take down the big guys, I could take down the kids in my own weight class with greater speed and power.

After my coach felt that I had mastered the takedown, he gave me another technique to work on. He said that I needed to learn how to escape from the bottom position. In wrestling, you start the 1st period on your feet, but the 2nd and 3rd period is the wrestler's choice. Depending on what they have mastered, a wrestler can choose neutral position (on their feet), top (where they start chest to back), or bottom (on hands and knees). If my opponent chose top, that meant I had to fight from the bottom to escape. This is where quickness comes in. If I could stand up quick enough from when the whistle blew, I could escape and take down my opponent.

I have found that this experience of wrestling in high school has helped me understand how to fight and to have courage in it. There will be times in your life when you are fighting against a bigger opponent—but you still have to join the battle.

There will also be times when your trials and tribulations are working hard to keep you down, and you will feel as if you are starting from the bottom—simply fighting to stand. But if you have the courage to fight and keep trying to escape, you will come out stronger.

We all have the courage in us to fight. And when we exercise that courage, we become a different individual, all together.

Are there circumstances in your life that you need to fight for, but you haven't found your courage yet? Dig deep and find the courage you need, then go out there and fight for what you believe in. It just might change your life.

"It's about having the **COURAGE** *to stand and fight for your life. Having the strength to go bravely in your own direction! Even if others walk away. You tread your own path!"*

~ FEARLESS MOTIVATION

CHAPTER 4

THE COURAGE
TO LET OTHERS IN

> *"If we are to shift our lives, we need to have the* **COURAGE** *to open the door, and allow the right people in."*

As I have done research on this chapter, what comes up in the search for the courage to let others in, is the courage to let go, the courage to forgive, and the courage to love. As I have thought about this, all these aspects of courage have been essential to my ability to let others in. I have had to let go of the fear of other people taking advantage of me. I have had to forgive those who have hurt me. And by having that courage to forgive, I have been given the ability to love. In the long run, I have learned that we need to overcome the fear that we can't be helped and believe that we are worth rescuing.

One morning, around 7:00 am, I was getting ready for school. Being eight years old, it does not take that long to get ready. As I was brushing my hair, there was a loud knock on the door, and I ran to answer it. All the adults were sleeping except my aunt, who was getting my cousins ready for school. I yelled through the door, and asked who it was.

The voice on the other side was loud and booming. It said, "SAN JOSE POLICE! OPEN UP!!"

I froze, like a deer in the headlights, for what seemed like an eternity. I didn't do or say anything—I just stood there, not knowing how to respond. I was always told not to open the door to the police.

As I stood there, the voice spoke again, "SAN JOSE POLICE! OPEN UP!!! OR WE WILL KICK IT OPEN ON THE COUNT OF THREE!!!"

Then I heard, "One.... Two.... Three!" BOOM—the door came flying open, which snapped me out of my trance and I took off running. I hid under our dining room table, totally terrified. The next thing I knew, a police officer grabbed me from under the table and sat me on our living room couch. The police went to the back bedrooms and brought all the adults out in handcuffs. My mom, stepfather, brother, his girlfriend, aunt and uncle, and all the kids—there were five of us—were all gathered together in the living room.

My cousins were screaming. They were terrified. I wasn't, though. I was still in shock, I guess. I remember the police asking the adults questions like, "Just tell us where the drugs are and it will be easy on you."

It took them a long time to find what they were looking for. During that time, I had asked if I could use the restroom. Thankfully, they said yes, and I was escorted to the bathroom. I remember walking past the television, and seeing that the movie *Beverly Hills Cop* was on. I didn't know what irony was back then, but I thought it was funny that I was, at that very moment, participating in a real life San Jose Cop experience—just like the television show. They even checked me before I entered the bathroom, to make sure I didn't have any drugs on me to flush down the toilet, and the officer stood close by as I relieved myself. It was very surreal.

All the adults in my house said they didn't even know what the cops were talking about. But just as they were saying that, a voice from one of the back rooms said, "BINGO!" An officer had found what they were looking for. They brought out the drugs, and all the cash, which they counted right there in front of us. From what they said, and what I could understand from listening in on the conversation, they found a lot of drugs in our house. And I don't recall how much money was there, but from the looks of what was on the table, it was a lot.

As they were getting ready to take everyone to jail, they had to decide what to do with the kids. They discussed putting us into foster care, until one of the officers said that they had nothing on my aunt and uncle, so we could stay with them.

They took my mom, brother, and stepfather to jail that day. My brother was only 17—turning 18 in a couple of months—and in a wheelchair. I gave him a hug and said goodbye. I felt anger towards my mom and stepfather. All of their bad choices brought us to this point and I was angry with them because of it. So I did not hug them—I just let them leave. I guess that maybe I saw it as a way of punishing them for all the hurt and pain they had caused our family.

After the police left, I remember the house had been destroyed. There was stuff everywhere—in every room. As we cleaned up, we found that the police did not even get all the drugs. It was a crazy mess.

That night, we watched the evening news, and they showed my mom and stepfather on television. From the news report, we learned that we had been just one of multiple drug raids that day. We also found out that one of my brother's friends had turned informant for the police, and had been wearing a wire while buying drugs from them—the cops had them on tape.

The police may have expected me to stay with my aunt and uncle, as they had discussed when arresting my immediate family members, but I was uprooted and sent to live with my dad and stepmom, instead. In most cases, it wouldn't have felt that this was a bad thing, because at my dad's house there was some sense of stability. But I had just watched as my mom, stepfather, and brother were handcuffed by the police, and taken to jail. And in my mind, they were taken from me because of their actions. I was angry with everyone, and I didn't want help from anyone. But moving into my dad's house, while still a difficult place to be, put me on a course that changed my life for the better.

How often do we freeze, or run away when people are trying to help us? I have had to learn how to forgive my mom, my stepfather, and my brother for all the pain that they have caused—and continue to cause.

Because of their choices, I was forced to leave their home and move in with my father. But because of that move, I had the chance of a better life. I was angry because of their poor choices, but as a result of those choices, my life turned out different in a positive way.

Looking back, I could have easily chosen to follow their example. But I had to fight my fears, and choose something better. I had to let go of thoughts that people were out to get me and take advantage of me, and have the courage to let people in who could help me. I had to have the courage to let go of my family's lifestyle, and let others step in where my parents didn't, and teach me how to stand tall.

"One of life's greatest moments was when I found the courage to let go of what I could not change, so I could change the things that mattered."

I could not change my family—only they had the power to change themselves. But their pride and distrust stopped them from allowing people in that could help them. I didn't want that same thing to happen to me. I learned that I had to be humble, and let others in who could help me out of the circumstances I grew up in.

Learning to trust others was one of the hardest things I have had to do through this experience. But once the trust came, I found that there was more to life than what I was seeing and experiencing from within my own family. I learned that there is actually good in the world—and people who are equally as good.

With the positive influences that I eventually let into my life, I discovered that I had a voice, that I could speak up for myself, and that the courage to do anything can be found in the gentle strength of another.

I have found that this life was not meant to be lived alone. Even though it is sometimes scary to let people in, once we do, we have an anchor to hold onto when everything else goes dark. When we can see ourselves through the eyes of those who love us, it bolsters us up, and gives us the courage to keep moving forward. If you struggle to let people in, I challenge you to reach out today to just one person and connect with them. Find your courage and let someone in.

"Opening yourself up to a person takes a huge amount of **COURAGE** *and trust. Even if you think you know, you never really know how they will react or respond and that will always be out of your control. In keeping them out, you keep the risk of disappointment and pain out, but in keeping them out, you keep the chance of acceptance and love out too. In the end, you really have to decide if the risk or the chance is more important to you and act accordingly."*

~ DOE ZANTAMATA

CHAPTER 5

THE COURAGE
TO JUMP

> *"When it feels scary to jump, that's exactly when you **JUMP**. Otherwise, you end up staying in the same place your whole life."*

As I watched my 18-month-old daughter jump from the couch to the ottoman, then from the ottoman to the couch, she would look at me and giggle every time she made it. I thought to myself *she has no fear*. But as I watched closer, just before she would jump, she would gear herself up for the leap. As if she was mustering up the courage.

Have you ever seen people who are successful, who seem to have the ability to do anything, and you thought to yourself they must be fearless? But take a closer look and you will see something a little different.

I surround myself with successful people. But I know that even successful people have fears. We don't see what it took for them to gain and maintain the success they have. The only difference is they have embraced the courage to jump. They take fear and allow it to motivate and move them. They have learned how to position themselves on the edge and make the jump, in spite of the fear they feel raging inside.

When I was young my dad taught me a very important life lesson. One day he checked me out of school for the day. He took me to a park and we walked around. As we were walking, we came to a playground built out of wooden logs. I asked him if I could play on it, and he said sure. So I started to play.

I was climbing up and going down the slide. While I was playing, I noticed this one log that stood taller than the rest. I decided to climb to the top of the log and stand on it. As I climbed up and stood on top of it, I felt the fear of being up so high start to creep in.

I was up really high, and looking down at the ground was scary. The ground seemed so far away.

As I stood there in fear, I called out to my dad. "Dad!" I said, "I am scared! Can you get me down?"

My dad said something I will never forget. He said "No! You got yourself up there, you can get yourself down."

"I am scared," I pleaded, hoping this would soften his heart.

"There is nothing to be scared about," he said. "Just jump."

Easy for him to say. He was a grown man and the jump was small to him. I was a kid—barley four feet tall. And the jump might as well have been a mile down. I begged him, but he still replied with a stern no. Then what he did next was crazy to me at the time.

He said he was leaving, and if I wanted to go home with him—I needed to jump. This was getting serious! I was not only scared to jump, I was also scared that I was going to be left on top of the log forever. I was fighting with my fears—which one was scarier—jumping or getting left? Getting left won out.

Now all I needed to do was jump. I told

myself I would count to three and then jump. I counted. One, two, three—nothing happened. My feet felt cemented to the log. I couldn't do it. I was watching my dad get farther and farther away from me.

I started to muster up some courage. I told myself, "I can do this! Just jump!"

I said that at least five more times. With all the fear of being left behind closing in on my mind, the only thing standing in my way was a jump. Again I mustered up every bit of courage I could find inside me and I jumped. The fall seemed eternal. Once my feet finally hit the ground I was overcome with joy. I had just conquered my fear and I was okay. I took off running towards my dad.

"I did it! I did it! I jumped!" I yelled to him.

He gave me a hug and smiled. Then he said to me, "You can do anything when you put your mind to it."

Would my dad have actually left me? I don't believe so. But he taught me a great lesson—a lesson I go back to all the time. That lesson gives me the courage to jump into everything I do. Because I jumped, I learned that no matter how scared I am, no matter how worried I can be, as long as I put my mind to it and jump—it will all work out. Even if I fail at things, at least I have tried and learned from trying. There are always lessons waiting to be learned, even—no, especially—in the failures of our lives.

My teenagers are constantly learning this lesson. I remind them that overcoming their fears is a matter of mindset. Sometimes they have to jump into opportunities to find out what they're made of, and to realize they can do it. Now days, kids have a hard time talking on the phone or ordering food at a restaurant. I challenge my kids every day to try something new—from trying new food, to speaking to a stranger, or just ordering food. Just like my dad, I find myself teaching my children it is their responsibility to get themselves out of the situations they got themselves into.

What situations do you find yourself in? Are you in a circumstance where you feel stuck, or where fear is holding you back from moving forward? Just count to three, tell yourself you can do it, and find your courage to jump. The joy you will feel in the accomplishment is far greater than the fear that is holding you back.

"Sometimes, we have to **STAND AND JUMP**, *even when we are afraid. By jumping, we can learn that fear is a construct of our own mind, and when we jump, we crush the fears that keep us stuck."*

~ TIFFANY FLETCHER

CHAPTER 6

THE COURAGE TO SPEAK

> *"Staying quiet to keep the peace can be a good thing, but if the peace has already been disturbed, staying quiet won't make anything better. Summon your* **COURAGE** *and speak up when you feel the need to."*
> ~ DOE ZANTAMATA

There have been many times in my life where I have had to stand up for myself because of the environment I grew up in. I had to stand up, and speak up, because I had no one who would do it for me. I had to learn, at a young age, to be strong. Not only did I have to learn to stand up for myself, but many times,

I also had to stand courageously and speak up for family members who didn't have the strength or courage to fight for themselves.

Living with my mom, I would only go to school when I was allowed to. I was kept home to watch younger kids. Because of this, school was often put on the back burner. When I did go to school, I had to get up at 4:30 a.m. to get ready and catch a bus at 5:30 a.m. But getting up in the middle of the night to make bottles and change diapers, which was more often than not my job because of the parties & drunken adults, made it hard to get out of bed. It also made it hard to focus.

I felt lost a good portion of the time. I didn't know where and what I was supposed to be doing. Getting behind in school and school work was hard, and it took a toll on me and my confidence and abilities. Unfortunately, because I was so behind, my teachers' opinions of me didn't help my confidence, and often made it worse. My freshman year in high school, I had an English teacher who told me that I was going to be a loser my whole life—that I would never amount to anything. And he could have been right—if I hadn't learned how to speak up for myself.

My brother doing drugs also took a toll on me. He had no idea how his personal yet damaging choices affected the rest of us, especially me. I was not happy about it. I just wanted him to stop—to make a different choice. But I didn't know how to even talk to him about it.

One night, my brother said that he was going to take a shower—but I knew what he was really doing. I had seen him do it before. He would run the water to try and fake people out. But I knew different. I knew the truth of what taking a shower meant for him. I still wanted to make sure, though. So I went outside, grabbed a stool so I could see, and put it under the bathroom window. As I stepped up on the stool and looked through the window, I saw my brother heating up a spoon and then tying his belt around his arm. He then put a needle in the spoon, sucked up what he liquified, put the needle in his arm, and pushed the drug into his vain.

I stepped down from the stool feeling both anger and sadness. I ran into the house and decided that I was going to tell him how I felt. This decision required a lot of me talking to myself, in order to gather the courage that I needed to confront him. As I was thinking through things, I also wanted to know where he was hiding his needles, so I went to his room and began to search. It took only ten minutes before I found them. I looked under the dresser, and there the needles were—in an orange bag, each topped with an orange cap. It looked like he had just bought the bag.

At that time, my brother started coming out of the bathroom. My natural reaction would have been to run away out of fear. But I was still so upset, that it gave me greater courage to confront him. When he came into the room, I sat the bag of needles on the bed. I looked at him and he looked at me, and then he looked at the needles on the bed.

"Where did you find those?" he asked.

"Under your dresser," I said. Before he could say anything else, I found the courage to speak boldly and unafraid, "You are my big brother, right?" I asked him.

He just nodded his head yes, without saying anything at all. I suspect he was probably a bit stunned that I was courageously standing up and opening my mouth. I am sure he could sense my confidence, which came from my passionate desire for him to stop ruining his life, as well as mine.

"Why are you doing drugs?" I asked. "What kind of example are you setting for me, your little brother? Do you want to die? Because what you are doing is going to kill you! You need to be a better example."

My brother just sat there, and even cried a little. "I'm sorry," he said.

It was so good to hear those words. I still remember that moment and treasure it as a defining moment in my life. It felt good to finally let my voice be heard. For years, I had watched silently as he was slowly killing himself with the drug addiction. And even though I couldn't make his choices for him, I learned that day that I have a voice and I found my courage to speak. Although it was a defining moment for me, I don't even know if my brother remembers because he was so high at the time. And even though having the courage to speak to my brother was more out of frustration, that frustration gave me the will to do so, and provided the courage I needed.

Do you have something that you are keeping inside that you wish people knew? I am sure that we all have things we wish we could say. It's important to find out what is stopping you from speaking, and find ways to push through that silence and find your own courage to speak. It's not easy, but it is definitely worth it. There is real healing that can come from having the courage to speak—even when the words are hard to say.

For example, when I was twenty-four years old, I finally let people know I had been molested when I was six. It took me 18 years before I found the words and the courage to share this secret because I lived in a family where these kind of secrets were best kept to yourself.

A child should feel safe in their own home—but I didn't. A child should be able to share their fears with their parents—but I couldn't. Because I never felt safe as a kid, I didn't feel I could trust any adult—my parents included. I worried that I was going to be teased or belittled because it had happened so many times before.

I have already shared how I was forced to watch as a woman was raped in my own home—and then I was teased about it. This was the reason I didn't tell my mom anything that happened to me. My mom didn't want to be seen as weak in front of the men in the house, even if her little boy suffered from what he witnessed. Because of her reaction, and the teasing from everyone else, I felt insecure about sharing my feelings and talking about the scary things that happened to me—especially confessing that I had been sexually abused myself.

The abuse took place in 1983, when my mom moved back to Utah for a few months, and we had several family members move in with us. At this time, my uncle (my mom's younger brother) was living with us. He shared a room with me in the basement. One night, my mom asked me to go take a shower in the downstairs bathroom. She asked my uncle to make sure I got clean.

As I showered, my uncle came into the bathroom, got into the shower with me, and started to touch my genitals. I remember being scared. He told me not to say anything and then proceeded to turn me around, bend me over, and use me for his sexual pleasure. I was crying and scared. I was afraid that there was no one that could help me or save me from this abuse. I felt that I just had to be strong and suffer through it until I could leave and go live with my dad for the summer.

I wish I could say it was a one time event, but it happened a few times. I just wanted to feel safe and protected—but the safety and protection never came. My stepfather and brother had a habit of calling me names like punk, sissy, fag, queer, and white boy. These were all meant to be derogatory. So telling anyone about the abuse at that time just wasn't a feasible option. I was sure I would be made fun of, teased, and called names—with no one to protect me. I felt I had no one to turn to. No one I could trust.

I felt so embarrassed. I now know it wasn't my fault. But I also know that I became a stronger person for working through it on my own, although I wouldn't suggest that approach. I know there are a lot of kids and adults who are not able to move past that kind of abuse because of the fear of how they would be looked at. Honestly, the fear of being seen differently caused me to push the experience down for a very long time.

Eventually, though, I finally did have the courage to tell someone. I received a call from my mom when I was in college, taking pre-law classes. She asked me to do some research for my uncle, who was in jail for molesting his daughter. It was then that the memory came flooding back to me. I told her no, I would not help him. She asked why. And I told her what he had done to me—I didn't hold back on the details. I was strong enough to handle the teasing.

But something happened that I didn't expect. My mother freaked out, and asked me why I never told her. I explained it was because I didn't want to be teased or called names. That may seem silly to some, but it was a real fear for me. The fear of being called names and being told that I was lying was very real to me. Even as I write this, all the memories and feelings come flooding back.

There will always be the right time when our courage to speak is needed. If not for ourselves, than for other people. Maybe if I would have said something sooner, my cousin would have been saved from the abuse. That uncle is now serving a life sentence in prison. I am so glad I found the courage to speak up about the sexual abuse I had suffered at his hand. I didn't allow this abuse to stop me from becoming who I am.

Elizabeth Smart said:

"Nobody is trial-free, but we have a choice. We can choose to allow our experiences to hold us back, and to not allow us to become great or achieve greatness in this life. Or we can allow our experiences to push us forward, to make us grateful for every day we have and to be all the more thankful for those who are around us."

I am not a victim. I am a survivor with the ability to change for the better. I choose to have courage, and I am grateful for the courage to speak.

If you find it hard to speak up in your own life, find simple opportunities to share your voice. The more you speak up, the easier it becomes. Your voice is important. Set aside your fear and find your courage to speak.

"COURAGE *gives us the power to change— not just to change ourselves, but the ability to empower that change in others."*

CHAPTER 7

THE COURAGE
TO CHANGE

*"We can still alter our course. It is NOT too late. We still have options. We need the **COURAGE** to change our values to the regeneration of our families, the life that surrounds us."*

~ OREN LYONS

In the beginning scene of the movie, *A Knight's Tale*, a young boy watches as a parade of knights march toward the arena where they will compete in a championship jousting tournament. As he watches the knights pass by, the young boy tells his father, with determination in his eyes, "I will become a knight someday." As he said this, he was laughed at by the people around him. They laughed because this boy and his father were poor and had no royal bloodline, which was required to be a knight.

One man said to the boy, "You might as well try to change the stars."

The boy, in his innocence, said to his father, "Can it be done? Can a man change the stars?"

The father then replied, "Yes, if he believes enough, a man can change anything."

Have you ever felt that way—felt like change was like moving a mountain or changing the stars? This was the story of my life. But the amazing thing about stories is that stories can be rewritten.

Tony Robbins said:

"*Change your Story—**Change your Life***"

How do we change our story? I believe that the only way to change our story is to change our mindset, or how we have been conditioned. When we learn to change our thoughts, we have the ability to rewrite our story into something better.

CHAPTER 7: THE COURAGE TO CHANGE

Have you ever walked into a room, and immediately felt that you were being judged, or categorized? Being Hispanic, people immediately assume that I speak Spanish. I don't. I know a few words, but having a conversation in Spanish is nearly impossible for me. This assumption most often happens when I go into a Mexican restaurant and the person taking my order starts asking me questions in Spanish.

Now, I can't escape my Hispanic heritage, nor would I want to. Being Hispanic is who I am. I even grew up in the stereotypical world of how Hispanic men are portrayed. Wikipedia shows that a very common stereotype of Hispanic/Latino males is that of the criminal gang member—or *cholo*. It is connected to the idea of Hispanics/Latinos being lower class and living in dangerous neighborhoods that breed this attitude of *cholo*.

Cholo and chola are terms often used in the United States to denote members of the Chicano gang subculture. These individuals are characterized by a defiant street attitude, a distinctive dress style, and the use of caló, which is a slang speech. In the United States, the term cholo often implies a negative connotation. And consequently, tends to be imposed upon a group of people, rather than being used as a means of self-identification. This leads to considerable ambiguity in the particulars of its definition. In its most basic usage, it always refers to a degree of indignity. This stereotype leads to a larger issue of the incarceration, race, and inequality of Hispanic males.

From the time that my mom left my dad, when I was four to the age of 15, I was conditioned to be a drug dealer, drug user, wife-beating alcoholic, gang member, and prison inmate. That was all I knew. It was all that I was taught and it is what was expected of me. But when events in my family life suddenly took a turn for the worst, I was given the opportunity to change.

One night, my mom was watching the news while I was in the kitchen getting something to eat. When all of a sudden, my mom cried out, "NO! NOT MY BABY!!!"

I ran into the family room to see my brother's face on TV. The news anchor said that 21 members of the notorious prison gang had been indicted, and that 10 of the members now faced the death penalty—one of the ten was my brother. That was why my mom screamed. Her son was going to die if found guilty of the crimes that he was being indicted for. She would constantly insist that he was innocent, but I knew that he wasn't; if truth be told she knew too.

A month had gone by since my brother had been indicted—and the mood in the house was one of depression and anger. The school year had come to an end, and I was headed to Utah to spend the summer with my dad. I was excited to leave. But I wanted to see my brother before I left to Utah. My mom and I headed downtown to the county jail where he was being held. We went through security and were lead by a sheriff to a private room, where we waited for them to bring him down from his cell.

The visiting room was just like you see in the movies. There were booths and a thick glass separating the visitors and the prisoners. But this room was only for those who were in the gang. There was a phone on each side of a 4" bulletproof glass with a grate over it. They wheeled my brother into the visiting room. He was wearing a red jumpsuit. His wrists were shackled to his waist. And even though he was in a wheelchair, he was also shackled at his ankles.

They undid one of his ankle shackles, and fastened it around a pole that was cemented to the floor—this is how dangerous they thought this paraplegic was. Then they unfastened one wrist shackle, so he could pick up the phone. We sat and talked with him this way for a while, which made it hard to see him at times. My mom talked to him first, for about 10 – 15 minutes, and then he asked to talk to me. Our conversation went something like this:

Brother: "Hey how are you?"

Me: "Fine. Just finished with the school year."

Brother: "That is good. I want to talk to you about something."

Me: "What is that?"

Brother: "I look at you and I see that you are confused about life. I want you to take a look at me. You do not want to be me. Look at where I am. This is no life for you. You need to get out of San Jose and go live with Dad."

Me: "I am leaving tomorrow for the summer."

Brother: "I mean live with him. Don't come back to San Jose. There is nothing but trouble here for you. You can make a life for yourself in Utah. Become something better than I am."

Me: (with a blank stare) "Ok, I will."

Oprah Winfrey said:
"Challenges are gifts that force us to search for a new center of gravity. Don't fight them, just find a new way to stand."

Do you have the courage to stand alone? When change is demanded, most people shy away from it because of fear of the unknown. Often the change we must make requires us to move forward alone—perhaps without a map or even an idea of how to change.

Mahatma Gandhi said:
"Sometimes not doing what's expected or following the crowd, is an act of courage. It's easy to stand in the crowd but it takes courage to stand alone."

Changing on your own will be hard. But you will not be alone for long because the right people will come along to assist you in your change. Stay resourceful and the resources will come.

When I left California at the age of 15, following the advice of my older brother, I had no idea what I was doing. He had asked me to do something drastic—to change my whole lifestyle, my whole upbringing—everything I was conditioned to do. But how does someone make such a stark change? And how does that change sink deep in order to obtain the life altering transition needed?

As I stepped off the plane at the Salt Lake City airport, I knew one thing—that changing my life was not going to be easy. Even though I left the crazy life I knew in California, I was going to live with my Dad who was an abusive alcoholic. I went from an environment of gangs, drugs, and murder, to one of angry alcoholics.

My change wasn't going to be easy. I was motivated and willing to do whatever it took. But in addition to the obstacles I already knew I was facing, I had one major problem.

Have you ever felt motivated about achieving a goal, but had no clue how it was to be accomplished—so doubt and fear took over?

That was my problem. I found myself lost and confused and scared. All I knew was that I had to do something different—and probably a lot of things different.

I remember sitting down one day and thinking about how I needed to change, and what I needed to do to make it happen. I came up with one thing—I had to change my environment as much as I could.

For change to happen, I needed to muster the courage to leave the 'old life' behind. I knew that I needed to stay away from the gang scene. But I am Hispanic, and the majority of the Hispanics in my area and school were affiliated with gangs. Because of this, I made the decision not to hang around my culture once school started.

It would not be easy. I still had no clue how to make it happen, and didn't even know if it was going to be possible. I feared I would not be accepted by any other group. I feared I would be looked down upon because I came from a poor and hostile environment. But I had set out to change my stars, and I was determined to make that happen. I decided that to change, I needed to find something I was good at—something to keep me busy and far away from the pull of falling back into what I knew. But what?

Sports was the answer. When I was nine, and still living in California with my mom, I asked her if I could play football. She told me I couldn't because I was too small and it was too expensive. So I played baseball. However, I never stopped wanting to play football.

Several years later, I asked my mom again if I could play football. She said yes, but I had to pay for it myself. I was ecstatic because I had the money. I had been mowing lawns and pulling weeds for weeks, and I had saved the money needed to play. My mom drove me to the football field and signed me up. I got my equipment (helmet, pads, and jersey with my number) and was excited to get started.

During my first football practice, I thought I knew more than the coaches on what position I should play. I wanted to be a running back just like Walter Payton of the Chicago Bears—my hero. But the coaches had a different position in mind for me. Thinking I was right, I argued with the coach. He then told me to stay after practice. After practice, I spent 20 minutes in the push-up position.

I learned a valuable lesson that day—never argue with the coach, it is his team. Ironically, I learned the position they wanted me to play (free safety), I was actually good at it, and I loved playing it. During the football season, I made some new friends who weren't gang members. They were athletes who came from a different part of San Jose. They taught me the real meaning of being part of a family and a team. Our football team was really good. We went undefeated and won the championship.

The next spring I tried out for the high school baseball team, and I made it. Once again, I had to come up with the money to play. This time I had a little help from my brother. But it was worth it to me. Athletics gave me three important things: a safe place to go, friends who were not breaking the law, and a greater dose of confidence.

It was the summer following this experience that I found myself in Utah—wanting to change—but not really knowing how. I clung to the one way I had already experienced an environmental change—sports. This became my new focus. I was entering my sophomore year of high school and would be attending a new school, where I knew no one.

I knew the football team would be holding summer workouts, so one morning I decided to head over to the school and find out what I could do to get on the team. Coming from a gang environment, even though I didn't belong to a gang, I dressed like a gang member. I walked out my front door with confidence, yet a little nervous. As I walked down the street I thought about what I would say to the coach.

Arriving at the school, the football team was practicing on the back field. As I walked up, I saw the head coach sitting under a tree. He did not notice me walking up, but the players did. As I got closer and closer to the coach, I felt more and more uncomfortable about what I was doing. That confidence I walked out the front door with was fading with every step. I felt out of place. The players were whispering and pointing.

I finally reached the coach. He looked up and said, "Can I help you?"

I told him I wanted to try out for the football team.

"You don't have to tryout," he said. "If you want to play, you are on the team."

"Well, I would like to play," I said.

"What position do you play?" he asked.

I told him free safety.

"You look like a running back," he said. "Let me see what you can do."

I was put on the team and was running back the rest of my high school career. As time went on, I proved to the team that I had what it took to play football. Those players who had stared and whispered that first day, slowly became my friends.

It takes courage to face your fears.
You will have to put yourself in
uncomfortable situations.

Nelson Mandela said:

"I learned that courage was not the absence of fear, but the triumph over it. The brave man is not he who does not feel afraid, but he who conquers that fear."

If I had allowed fear to control me, I would not have been able to change my environment or my story.

Courage to change is not easy. You will stumble, and you will fall—and you will make mistakes. But if you keep believing, change *will* happen. Have faith in yourself and faith in the little changes. Also, have the courage to trust others to help you.

The courage to change begins with seemingly small steps that remain consistent. I encourage you to evaluate your life, and decide where changes need to be made. Then take one small step today toward that new direction. If you make one small positive change daily, overtime, you will see big results. So find your courage, and make the change.

"When we find ourselves in the uncomfortable world of change, we will also find there are people ready to help make the process of changing comfortable, as long as we have the **COURAGE** *to trust them."*

CHAPTER 8

THE COURAGE
TO *trust*

> *"To trust is to be courageous, because not everyone is worthy of your trust. You will only know they aren't trustworthy after you have trusted them. To go into the world and trust others, that needs* **COURAGE**.*"*
>
> ~ **SOLITARY SURVIVOR**

Trusting others does not come easy when you are trying to change. Especially when every person from your former life has proven to be dishonest, manipulative, and selfish. When a person has been let down by others on a consistent basis, finding the courage to trust again needs to come from first trusting yourself.

Golda Meir said:

> *"Trust yourself to create the kind of self that you will be happy to live with all your life. Make the most of yourself by fanning the tiny inner sparks of possibility into flames of achievement."*

What I found was that because I had been through so many trials and tribulations, I was constantly living in survival mode. I was observant to my surroundings and I learned who I could trust and who I couldn't. When someone let me down, I just internalized it, and tried to handle it on my own. But I discovered that when I found the courage to trust people—people sometimes surprised me.

Leaving California, I had to learn how to trust the new influences that were coming into my life. I came from an environment where everyone around me would lie, cheat, and steal to get gain. They didn't care how it affected others, they just wanted more for themselves. Because of this, I always had my guard up. I found myself constantly questioning the intentions of these new influences. I wondered when they would get what they wanted and walk away. I wondered why they were so willing to help me. As time went on, I realized there are people who truly care to help others develop, without any benefit to themselves. No praise. No glory. No money. Nothing.

These people showed me I could trust them. Because of that trust, I wanted them to be able to trust me, so I began to change. I began to be trustworthy because I didn't want to lose these people in my life. Therefore creating a wonderful cycle in trusting and being trustworthy. When you find these types of people in your own life, they also need to know you can be trusted and you are committed to your own change.

Coach Tekano was one of these people for me. He trusted me, and therefore I wanted to be worthy of that trust. Walking onto the football field that day, I didn't know what to expect. I had no idea how I was going to be treated. I realize that the coach didn't care what I looked like—he was taking a chance on me. He was placing trust where he could have, by one look at me, placed discontent. With Coach trusting me, I found myself wanting to be my best to prove to him that his trust was not misplaced.

Have you ever trusted someone, and their positive influence encouraged you to be better than you thought you were? That is what Coach did for me—he made me better. His influence didn't just make me better, it introduced me to other influences—influences like John.

Lolly Daskal said:
"Leaders with influence: Give when they don't have to. Care for others. Grow continuously. Live authentically. Empower others. Manage hardships. Serve with humility."

John was that kind of leader. I met John in my junior year of high school, and he quickly became my mentor. John would take his two young boys to watch our team play football. My junior year, I played on the varsity team as a running back. John was amazed that someone my size was playing running back, until he saw me run the ball.

He later described the experience like this: "I saw this little guy go for a 10 – 15 yard gain and get pummeled by a defender, and then he jumped up and ran back to the huddle. He was like the Energizer Bunny." He told his boys he would, "…like to meet that kid."

Eventually, we did meet. I started dating his sister, who lived with him. On one particular night, I went to visit her—I remember it being dark. I walked up to the door and knocked. John answered the door, and with a big smile, invited me in. John could have taken one look at me and my appearance, and decided I had no future and brushed me off. Instead, he did something I never saw coming. He invited me into his home.

We sat down at his kitchen table and shared some milk and cookies. (Who does that?) John took an interest in me, and he gained my trust. He asked about my life, and he asked about my future. His care and influence didn't stop at that kitchen table over a plate of cookies and a glass of milk. No, John gave me my first suit. Along with which came some advice on how my outward appearance needed to reflect how I felt on the inside. He taught me how to take pride in myself.

Most importantly, John taught me how to influence others. When our aim for change is good, we meet good people. And when we put the past aside and have the courage to trust these good people, they will help us along our way to change.

Jim Rohn said:
"Get around people who have something of value to share with you. Their impact will continue to have a significant effect on your life."

Who influences you to do better—to become better?

I didn't have the resources that my friends had, but I was resourceful enough that I knew how to adapt to my environment.

Eric Thomas said:
"When we are resourceful, the resources will appear."

As I became more humble about changing, I was able to see the resources. By doing so, my courage to trust others gave me more resources and the encouragement to keep on making those changes that were shaping me into someone different—someone so much better. Your own courage and ability to trust others will give you the same kind of resources and encouragement to change. It is a remarkable thing that if we find the courage in one area of our life, it spills over into other areas as well.

John has always been a great resource to me. When I decided to make another significant change in my life, I looked to him for guidance. Boy did he provide it! He gave me the foundation for leadership. He showed me how to see the value in others. He taught me to look for the best leaders and then emulate what they were doing until I figured it out myself. But the single most important thing I learned from him—is that it was not all about me.

John's lessons on leadership were extremely valuable, as I prepared to leave on a mission for my church to New Jersey. It was the morning of July 1st, I was at work and received some devastating news that a dear friend of mine had committed suicide the day before. As you can imagine, after receiving this news, I wasn't feeling well. So I went home early. On my way home, I decided to visit my cousin. While I was at my cousin's house, his girlfriend showed up looking for me. She told me that I needed to go to her house, as soon as possible.

"Why?" I asked.

She told me her mom needed to tell me something. But she didn't say what. I had no idea why I was going, but I went to her home anyway. As soon as I entered the door, I met her mother.

"Go downstairs," she said, "and I will come talk to you." Again, there was no explanation. I was just told to go downstairs.

I was now worried. I walked downstairs like I was told, but came right back up.

"What is going on?" I asked.

She looked at me with tears in her eyes. "Something has happened with one of your family members," she said.

I instantly thought of my brother. "Is it my brother?" I asked.

"No," she said.

"Is it my mom?" I guessed a second time.

"No," she said again.

"It's my dad, isn't it?" This time, I just felt

in my gut that this was the right answer.

"Yes," she said.

"He is dead, isn't he?" I asked her the question, but I already knew the answer.

"Yes," she said.

She then explained that my dad was coming back from doing a drug deal with his "lady friend." They were both high, and the lady was driving. They were traveling on the highway when the lady fell asleep and the car drifted across the median into oncoming traffic. They ran head-on into a semi, killing both of them instantly.

After receiving this news, I had my own little freak-out session. It was a lot to take in. First my good friend, and now my dad…both gone! Life seems to always have a way of throwing us curve balls. It is how we receive those pitches that truly decide the fate of our game.

After I had calmed down from the initial shock, John's leadership lessons came into play. My mom and sister would need a phone call, letting them know what had happened. Because John had taught me about being selfless, I applied that lesson and took on the difficult task of making those phone calls. I was also in charge of the funeral. It would have been easier to sit in the seats and just mourn my dad. Instead, I knew it would be easier for others if they saw my strength, so I made it about the people I cared about. I remember feeling sad, but I was also grateful I was able to handle it without breaking down.

That fateful day I sat down with John at his kitchen table, eating cookies, I could have dismissed all he had to say. I could have decided I was too cool to listen to some "old" guy. What if I had? How would that have affected me and those I love? I am certain I would not have been equipped to not only handle these two deaths in my life, but to be the leader my family needed at my father's funeral.

The courage to trust allows us to overcome the negative attitudes and fears that talk us out of change—those voices in our head that keep us stuck in a never-ending cycle of destruction. The courage to trust gives us the courage to believe in ourselves, and believe that we can handle anything that comes our way. And best of all, the courage to trust keeps us focused and in the game, because someone else is cheering us on from the sidelines.

Do you have someone who cheers you on from the sidelines? If not, I encourage you to reach out, even if it's hard, and find someone to connect with—a mentor, a friend, a co-worker, anyone really. There are billions of people on this planet. Go find your people! The courage to trust may be one of the hardest kinds of courage, but it is also the one that is the most worth the effort.

"The **COURAGE** *to trust others gives us the ability to believe in something more meaningful than ourselves."*

CHAPTER 9

THE COURAGE
TO BELIEVE

> "When you **BELIEVE** in a thing,
> believe in it all the way, implicitly
> and unquestionably."
>
> ~ WALT DISNEY

Are you where you belong? Are you doing what you want to do and what you are meant to do? As a business coach I find that most of my students have been through a lot of ups and downs in their lives. They are looking for an opportunity that will take them to the next level. But something keeps them from taking that step. In all my experience I have found that "something" is a belief in themselves.

We can't have big success unless we believe we can do it. On the outside my students appear to have it all together. But inside a battle is raging. They lack the confidence and courage to stand out. Their past failures lead them to believe they will fail again. This thought process leads them to self-sabotage. Self-sabotage happens when we listen to all the voices from the past that say...we are not good enough...smart enough...talented enough...we are too short...too tall...too fat... too poor.

The courage to believe in ourselves begins with an understanding that our past, no matter the pain, has prepared us to overcome the challenges before us. We wouldn't be who we are without the struggles of our past that have made us stronger. Understanding this, changes our negative thoughts to thoughts of empowerment. Doing this consistently brings growth.

Caroline Myss said: " To love yourself, truly love yourself, is to finally discover the essence of personal courage, self-respect, integrity and self-esteem. These are the qualities of grace that come directly from a soul with stamina."

Growing up I was beat down physically, mentally, spiritually, and emotionally. I never felt like I belonged anywhere. Whenever I worked up the courage to try something new I would hear the voices of my mom, dad, brother and stepfather telling me I was too small or too weak. They would constantly put me down by calling me names like faggot, queer, punk, stupid, and sissy, in both English and Spanish (I guess this was their way of teaching me a second language). Because I was constantly being put down I often felt like I had to prove myself to everyone.

As a 13-year-old I lived in a one bedroom apartment filled with cockroaches with four other people (my mom, stepfather, little sister and new born brother). I had to grow up fast because I was constantly put in charge of my younger siblings. It was my responsibility to get up in the middle of the night to change diapers and get prepare bottles. There were nights I remember getting up to prepare a bottle and my mom and stepfather would be in our kitchen smoking crack. They would not pay any attention to me because they were so high. There were days I wasn't allowed to go to school because I had to take care of kids. If the house wasn't cleaned and the kids weren't dressed for the day I got in trouble. I felt like I did everything but also felt the it was never enough. I was constantly treated like I was not capable of anything, except being a babysitter. I was never allowed to go anywhere with friends because it was to inconvenient.

Growing up in that environment, how did I find the courage to believe in myself? It was the little things. When I was allowed to attend school I would take frustration out in my PE class. I would push myself to be the best at whatever we played. The teachers would tell me, "great hustle," "way to push." "you are fast." It gave strength to endure what I was facing at home. I wanted to be something more, but I didn't actually believe I could.

I had to overcome a great deal to find the courage to believe in myself. I believe my journey started when I started to believe in God. I grew up with a belief in God's existence, but the idea that He is actually aware of me was a very foreign concept. I found my faith in God when I was 17 and in my Junior year in High School. Many of the friends I had surrounded myself with had testimonies of God. They seemed happy all the time. Because of my home life and the many struggles there, I had little to no happiness in my life.

Gordon B. Hinckley said:

"We are involved in an intense battle. It is a battle between right and wrong, between truth and error, between the design of the Almighty on the one hand and that of Lucifer on the other. For that reason, we desperately need moral men and women who stand on principle... The time has come for us to stand a little taller...This is a season to be strong. It is a time to move forward without hesitation, knowing well the meaning, the breadth, and the importance of our mission. It is a time to do what is right, regardless of the consequences that might follow. We have nothing to fear. God is at the helm."

This battle was definitely raging inside of me and I was tired of feeling like I was on the wrong side. Because of the encouragement from my brother, I was already looking for ways to change. I had started school sports, but still felt like I was missing something. One day I was given the opportunity to change sides.

My home life with my dad was hardly any better than what I left behind in California. While I wasn't required to get up with babies, my dad was an alcoholic and would get violent. Many times I had to step in-between him and my stepmother when they would fight. I constantly felt like I was the glue holding my family together. There was one day I didn't want to go to my Biology class, or be at school at all for that matter. I didn't want to go home either. As I stood by the door of the Biology class room my friend Mark came up to me and asked, "What's up?" I told him I didn't want to go to class. I am not sure if Mark could feel that I was struggling with something, but he had the courage to invite me to seminary.

In Utah, youth of the Church of Jesus Christ of Latter Day Saints have the opportunity to have a free class period and attend a seminary class during school. Looking at Mark and not completely understanding what he was asking, I reluctantly agreed. That day I learned that Heavenly Father has a plan. He cares about us. I learned about Jesus Christ. I learned about a man named Joseph Smith, who was a prophet. I learned about a book of scripture called The Book of Mormon. During my time in the class I felt good and peaceful. My conversion was not immediate, it took a couple of months to realize that the peace I felt came from feeling the Holy Ghost. Eventually I converted to The Church of Jesus Christ of Latter Day Saints.

The businessman, Mohamed Al-Fayed said:
"The most important thing is God's blessing and if you believe in God and you believe in yourself, you have nothing to worry about."

My life situation did not change overnight, in fact it got worse. My family didn't change what they were doing. I was put down for believing in God, and converting to a different religion. These insults came from the people closest to me, as they always had before. However, whenever we go against the grain, or strive to become better than we were, there will always be people who try to knock us down. Don't let that discourage you? There will always be someone to tell you that you are making the wrong choice. I knew this slander would come…my whole life it came. Why would this be any different. With my relationship with, and belief in God, I found the strength to cope with all the chaos and personal attacks. As I was given the strength to endure, I began to have a stronger belief in myself. That led to me seeing people differently. I started to believe that I could be a greater influence for good. I started to believe in something bigger than myself.

Nick Vujicic said:
"The greatest rewards come when you give of yourself. It's about bettering the lives of others, being part of something bigger than yourself, and making a positive difference."

Because I missed so much school in my younger years, I did not really learn how to read until I was 20-years-old. In fact, even now somethings I am uncomfortable reading out loud. In conjunction with my struggles to read, my vocabulary wasn't extensive. This was one of the things that made me feel inferior. All my friends would get good grades in high school, where I struggled to maintain a C average. You can imagine how this would play on my confidence as the idea of writing this book came to mind. It has been ten years that I have listened to the voices telling me I was not qualified....that I wasn't smart enough. Finally, when I dug deep to find the courage to start this book, I have come to realize that all my life's hardships, all that I have been through, can be used to assist others in their struggles. I have come to understand that my story is bigger than myself. Writing this book has been hard. I have had to face things I never wanted to remember. On top of that when people edit my writing, I have to fight those emotions that are telling me I am not good enough. I have to remember that this is what I am supposed to do with my life story. I am supposed to lift and encourage others on the path.

"It takes **COURAGE** *to keep walking*
when the path is obscured by confusion.
Trust. Believe. And just keep walking.
The way will be revealed!"

~ SUE KREBS

CHAPTER 10

THE COURAGE TO <u>STAY</u>

> "**COURAGE** *means working on a relationship, to continue seeking solutions to difficult problems, and to stay focused during stressful periods."*
> ~ DENIS WAITLEY

When we are going through change, it becomes hard to see the people we love continue to struggle. There will come a time when you will recognize the difference in yourself, and you will want to bring those loved ones up with you to also experience the difference. You will make decisions that you feel are right for you, but it may not be the right time for others.

Just a month before my senior year was about to start, I had a falling out with my dad and stepmother. I was tired of the drinking and the fighting. I was also tired of being the referee. So I made a decision to move out of my parents' house.

Not knowing where I was going to live, I called the Roberts family. They had been my refuge once before and I hoped they could help. They took me in with open arms. But they didn't just take me in—they had to make room for me. They had seven kids already, four boys and three girls. So adding another kid to the mix was not an easy feat. But they did it anyway.

I learned a great deal from Mark Sr. He taught me many things about respect—not only for myself, but for the women in my life. He showed me that his wife was his queen, and that she was the most important person in his life. He showed me that being a father meant that he was a man who earned the respect of his children and didn't just demand that respect. He showed me that providing a happy home is important for the health of the family. Although I was not his kid, he accepted me as if I was.

Julie Roberts, the mom of the home, showed me that a mother is someone who cares and nurtures her children. She showed me that a mother's love is unconditional.

Living with the Roberts was like a sanctuary for me—and it was refreshing. There wasn't yelling everyday, like there was in my own home. Sure, it was still loud with that many teenagers. But it was a happier place to be. They paid attention to me and what I was interested in. They listened, and they cared.

Victor Frankl said:

"Love is the only way to grasp another human being in the innermost core of his personality. No one can become fully aware of the very essence of another human being unless he loves him. By his love, he is enabled to see the essential traits and features in the beloved person; and even more, he sees that which is potential in him, which is not yet actualized but yet ought to be actualized. Furthermore, by his love, the loving person enables the beloved

> *person to actualize these potentialities. By making him aware of what he can be and of what he should become, he makes these potentialities come true."*

My time with the Roberts family only lasted five months. Not because they kicked me out, nor was it because I didn't feel welcomed or loved. My dad was going through a hard time. He had separated from my stepmom and was still addicted to drugs. He desperately needed help. I thought I could be a good influence on him, so I decided to go back and live with him. Telling the Roberts I was leaving was very hard—and leaving the comfort of their home was even harder. One of the hardest parts for me was that my dad and I did not have a place to live. We lived out of his car sometimes, or we stayed with family members. Sadly, some of those family members did drugs right along with him.

My influence on my dad had the reverse effect. One night while we were staying at my cousins' house, my dad and cousins were drinking and doing drugs. I was tired of seeing what they were doing to themselves, so I decided to walk outside to get away. As

I was walking, I ran into some missionaries, one of which had taught me.

I really don't remember the conversation, but I remember feeling that being with my dad was bad for me—that I was in the wrong place. The influence I thought I could be on my dad was having the reverse effect on me. Even though I knew my dad needed to change, he was the only one who could make those changes, and he had to decide when, where, and if those changes would take place. I had to come to terms that my dad wasn't ready to change, and I needed to move on.

There are times when the courage to stay is just merely planting seeds. That was what I was doing for my dad—because he wasn't ready.

We all have circumstances in our lives where we have to make the decision whether we are going to stay or go. Sometimes the courage to stay means you go outside of your comfort zone, and stay with a family that is not your own. And sometimes the courage to stay means that you stay in a difficult situation for only a season, and plant those seeds of change for a later harvest. Either way, the courage to stay is needed. In the end, we have to choose the soil where we are going to plant our own feet and stay—so those seeds of change can grow in our own life.

I challenge you to honestly review your life and see if there are circumstances where the courage to stay applies to you. Where have you chosen to stay? And where are you choosing to plant your feet?

Although we need to have the courage to stay, to plant seeds and to hopefully make a situation better, we also need to understand that if we can't make the situation better, we equally need the courage to jump.

"Knowing when to walk away is wisdom. Being able to is **COURAGE**. *Walking away with your head held high is dignity."*

~ LIFEHACK

CHAPTER 11

THE COURAGE
TO *RUN*

> *"If you can't fly then run, if you can't run then walk, if you can't walk then crawl, but whatever you do you have to* **KEEP MOVING FORWARD.***"*
>
> ~ DR. MARTIN LUTHER KING JR.

In 2009, I had a group of friends who liked to compete in triathlons. They invited me to get involved.

My first reaction was, "Um, NO!"

All I knew about triathlons were the Ironman triathlons. And I was no Ironman. I could run, but biking and swimming were something totally different. That meant I had to train for all three.

They finally sold me on the crazy idea by telling me we would "just" be doing a sprint distance triathlon. For those of you as naive on the subject as I was, this means you swim 400 – 500 yards, bike 12 – 15 miles, and then end with a 3.1 mile run. Clearly not an Ironman, so I figured I could do it.

I trained only about a month before my first triathlon. It went about the way I expected it to. It didn't take long for me to figure out I enjoyed running a lot, biking wasn't bad, but I loathed swimming. Race day came and I found I enjoyed myself—perhaps because my favorite part was last.

Then one of those friends who got into the triathlon world, got another hairbrained idea and we wanted me to join. You see, he had enlisted in the Army and wanted to run a marathon before he began basic training. When he initially asked me, my immediate response was, "No." He pleaded with me. He told me I was a great runner and pointed out that running was my favorite part of being a triathlete anyway. He even went as far as to tell me it would be easy. I gave into his flattery and reluctantly accepted his invitation. That's when he told me the race was in three weeks.

I had never run a marathon, so I had no idea that people trained hard for these. My friend had been training for months—I had three weeks. I sort of figured that since I loved running, a marathon really might be easy. I didn't anticipate how very different a marathon would be from a triathlon. Marathons are all about endurance—and being fueled and hydrated.

The day of the marathon came. I was excited and nervous all rolled into one. Although the race didn't start until 6:30 a.m., we had to catch a bus to the starting line at 3:30 a.m. It was a 45 minute bus ride up the windy canyon. Once we got to the starting line, we had time to "relax," whatever that means. Perhaps for seasoned marathoners relaxing is a thing. But for me, the newbie, I just paced. I tried to loosen up my muscles and stay warm. After what seemed an eternity, it was finally time to start the race.

We lined up and the gun went off. I had no plans to run to win, but at the sound of the gun my competitive nature kicked in and I took off like winning was my intention.

I eventually settled into my run and was feeling great coming up on mile three. Suddenly, my foot landed in a groove on the road and it tweaked my ankle. It hurt for a bit, but the pain went away very quickly.

Mile after mile my confidence grew. It was clear I wasn't going to win, but this marathon thing seemed easy. I began to wonder why I stuck to triathlons for so long. I had no problems reaching the halfway point (13.1 miles).

Mile 19, I was still feeling great!

I hit mile 20 in three hours. I said to myself, "I can do this marathon in under four hours." Then came mile 21.

If you talk to marathon runners, many of them will reference the phrase "hitting a wall." This means, as you might guess, an inability to move forward. Most runners hit this metaphorical wall at mile 20. I hit mine at mile 21. And boy, did I hit it! I hit it so hard I felt like I got run over by a dump truck. Pain shot from my head to my toes. The running stride I had going, came to a near crawl. Oh, and remember when I said I tweaked my ankle near mile three? That pain came back with a vengeance and it stayed with me to the end.

I only had 5.2 miles left. Normally, I could run five miles in about 40 minutes. But, for the next hour and 50 minutes, I was reevaluating my life choices and was flirting with quitting. Although I was moving slower than a turtle, and my body was in the worst pain it had ever felt, at least I was still moving. With every small step, no matter how small, and the encouragement of every person who passed me by, asking if I was OK—I was getting closer to the finish line.

Let me tell you why my body shut down so bad.

1. I only trained for three weeks, and my longest run was 15 miles. Most marathoners' longest run before a race is 20 – 21 miles, a couple of times. And they train 3 – 5 months before a race.

2. I did not hydrate the day before and did not carb load. The body needs fuel.

3. I had the wrong shoes. There are shoes that are used for long distance, and there are shoes used for sprinting. I had the latter.

As I ran those last miles, my mind was all over the place. I was working through some serious thoughts. Thoughts like: "Am I going to die?" to "Am I going to be paralyzed?" I was certain it would be one of the two.

I finally got to mile 26 and thought, "I am done. Where is the finish line?" Then it hit me—a marathon is 26.2 miles. I still had .2 miles to go. I felt like someone had punched me in the gut. I wanted to be done so I told myself, "You've got this! Just finish."

Just before crossing the finish line, I saw my friend who invited me to run, and I said, "I hate you! I will never do this again."

As I crossed the finish line, I started crying like a baby. I had just put my body through the worst pain it had ever been through.

The marathon was, no doubt, tough. But after sitting in a car for 30 minutes driving home, getting out was even harder. When I got home and tried to get out of the car, my body wouldn't move. My brain was telling my legs to move, but they wouldn't. I had to summon the little strength I had left just to get out of the car. With nothing left in the tank, I crawled into my house on my hands and knees.

It took me two whole weeks to recover from that marathon.

Remember when I said I would never run a marathon again? I lied! I have done it again, not just once, but nine more times. Every marathon has had its challenges, and I have had to work through those challenges and just keep running. Running has become my stress reliever. It helps me to refocus, and at times, inspires me to do something crazy— like write a book. Sometimes, you just have to run with it.

When life is going well, and you feel like everything is falling into place, then all of a sudden you are hit with a setback that slows down your progress—what do you do? How do you keep going?

"Crossing the starting line may be an act of courage, but crossing the finish line is an act of faith. Faith is what keeps us going when nothing else will. Faith is the emotion that will give you victory over your past, the demons in your soul, and all of those voices that tell you what you can and cannot do and can and cannot be."

~ JOHN BINGHAM

While training for my fourth marathon, and about four weeks to race day, I was right on track with my training schedule. Then the inevitable happened—I suffered a setback. Having ten children, the odds were stacked against me that someone would bring home one sickness or another. And sure enough, two of them got colds. One night I felt my own cold come on. I started having cold sweats, headaches, and weakness throughout my body.

When I get sick, I often tell my wife I am dying. So she has learned to kind of ignore it. But this time I really felt like I was dying. As the days went on, the mucus was draining into my lungs. One night, I woke up and felt like I was drowning. So my wife and I decided it was time for me to go to the doctor.

The doctor examined me and when she checked my lungs, she heard a gurgling sound. "You have pneumonia," she said.

"What?" I said. "Wait, I can't have pneumonia. I have a marathon in four weeks."

"Well you need to rest, and shouldn't be running," she said. She gave me a shot of antibiotics and pills I had to take for ten days. She then said that I had to take it easy with my runs for the next ten days, with no high mileage.

Four weeks before a marathon is when you should be increasing the mileage of your runs, but I was sort of sidelined. I was stuck running only five to six miles a day.

I struggled through the first couple of runs because my energy was so low. I had to stop and rest, and then pick up my run again. It was very frustrating. I knew I had to get at least one big run in before race day. I planned to do 20 miles, two weeks before the marathon. That run turned out to be only 18 miles. Once again, I was left to brain powering my way across the finish line.

Over the years, I have met people who have been through some of the toughest trials in life. Trials that should have stopped them from functioning. But where some people would have just quit on life, they keep fighting.

My adopted brother, Barney Nelson, has had two liver transplants, due to a disease called Ulcerative Colitis. This disease left him dead, for just a few minutes, on an operating table. But the doctors were able to revive him.

He could have just given up the fight, but what he did next has inspired many people, including himself, to keep moving.

In his own words he states:

"For me, that was the day I was first introduced to Ulcerative Colitis. A not so fun opportunity to learn the geographical location of all the restrooms of the cities that I visit.

I have always loved to travel. And having Ulcerative Colitis made it super, SUPER hard to travel. Simply from the fact that when it's time to go, you will have only a brief moment to locate and find a restroom, before you explode.

I had a choice. I could let this beat me and keep me chained to my home restroom. However, I choose to fight the good fight and live my dream. I wanted to travel so that's what I did! I went to Peru and then to Paris and I did not let my condition stop me. I did not let fear hold me back. I wish I could say that it was all rainbows and sunshine after I faced my fears."

~ BARNEY NELSON

Since his second liver transplant, Barney and I have run many races together. Every time I see him running up a mountain it brings tears to my eyes, because he never gives up. He continues to have the courage to run up the mountain.

Dean Karnazes said:

> *"The Marathon is an opportunity for redemption. Opportunity because the outcome is uncertain. Opportunity because it is up to you, and only you, to make it happen."*
>
> **~ RUNNERSWORLD**

Are there moments in your life where you have hit a wall, of sorts, and have the choice before you of whether to quit or to keep moving forward? I challenge you to evaluate your circumstances and see if there are places where you are choosing to quit rather than run. Decide if it's important enough to you. And if quitting isn't an option, find your courage to run. Then when you wake up to face tomorrow, face it with the courage to stand tall.

"Any fool can run towards the light. It takes a master with **COURAGE** *to turn and face the darkness and shine his own light there."*

~ **LESLIE FIEGER**

CHAPTER 12

THE COURAGE TO STAND TALL

> *"Don't let anyone ever break your soul. You have to stand on your own two feet and stand up for yourself. There are those that would give anything to see you fail, but you must never give them the satisfaction. Hold your head high, smile and* **STAND TALL**.*"*
>
> **~ LIFEHACK**

The Courage to Stand Tall is our ability to overcome whatever life throws our way. There are those around us who want us to stay small and they try to accomplish this by tearing us down. There are those, who, when we stumble, fall, and fail, want to keep us from standing back up again. They make fun of us and tell us we can't do great things. These types of people can be found all around us, and it is because of this that I have summoned all my own courage, and have written this book. Courage is what it takes to keep getting up again. And standing tall is what it takes to prove that nothing and no one can keep you down.

I have witnessed, and been a part of, some truly horrific things. It took everything I had to become the person I am today. But being who I am is not just for me. It is for my children. It is for you the reader, and for anyone who hears and relates to my story. In sharing my story, I hope to show you the power of courage—that it can change you, to make you better than you were yesterday. I have had many people in my life step up and show me how to stand tall. It is now my responsibility to help others do the same.

CHAPTER 12: THE COURAGE TO STAND TALL

Recently, my good friend Mark passed away from a sudden heart attack. He was only 41. Mark left a lasting impression on many people's lives. At his funeral, the stories shared were stories of his willingness to inspire. His boys talked about their dad as their hero, and someone they aspired to be like.

One quote that was shared sums up the kind of man Mark was. He said, *"Who cares about tomorrow? Who cares about yesterday? All that is demanded of you is to win the day."*

Mark taught his boys that this meant to have an excellent day at school or work. This also means to have an excellent day of rest. This means, every hour of every day, be there. BE PRESENT. Don't think about the past—the *what ifs*. Just think about today, get up and do your work.

Another story that Mark's wife, Annie, shared was of when a friend came over just after Mark's passing. Annie, understandably, began to cry. Her youngest son, who was playing a video game, called out, "Mom, we got this!"

Through Mark's youngest son, he continued to inspire strength and courage in others.

My dear friend Mark was a great example to me. Even in a time of mourning, he inspired me to be a better father, husband, and leader.

I would say to those who struggle with addiction, depression, or abuse in all its forms, "YOU GOT THIS!!!" You are courageous.

When you are courageous, you need to make small changes, and you need to focus on the small accomplishments—everyday. Even making your bed can be a small accomplishment.

A few years ago, an Admiral gave a powerful speech on making your bed.

Admiral William H. McRaven was the Admiral's name. His speech was called, Make Your Bed. I love how he shares what happens when you make your bed. He said:

"Every morning in basic SEAL training, my instructors, who at the time were all Vietnam veterans, would show up in my barracks room and the first thing they would inspect was your bed. If you did it right, the corners would be square, the covers pulled tight, the pillow centered just under the headboard and the extra blanket folded neatly at the foot of the rack—that's Navy talk for bed.

It was a simple task—mundane at best. But every morning, we were required to make our bed to perfection. It seemed a little ridiculous at the time, particularly in light of the fact that we were aspiring to be real warriors, tough battle-hardened SEALs, but the wisdom of this simple act has been proven to me many times over.

If you make your bed every morning, you will have accomplished the first task of the day. It will give you a small sense of pride, and it will encourage you to do another task and another and another. By the end of the day, that one task completed will have turned into many tasks completed. Making your bed will also reinforce the fact that little things in life matter. If you can't do the little things right, you will never do the big things right."

(https://jamesclear.com/great-speeches/make-your-bed-by-admiral-william-h-mcraven)

Tiffany Fletcher wrote:

> *"Sometimes we have to get out of bed and simply stand on our own two feet in order to win the race. In the end, the winner is not the one who gets there the fastest. The winner is the one who has the courage to keep on standing."*

From the day we are born, we are conditioned to certain behaviors due to what our parents teach us, both through words and actions. For me, the teaching was to be a wife beating, alcohol drinking, drug dealing, drug addict. In addition to being a murdering gang member, prison inmate, and sex addict. But that is not who I am. I have broken free from the ropes that tried to bind me.

In the preface of this book, I shared a story called *The Elephant Rope*. I want to share that story again.

THE ELEPHANT ROPE

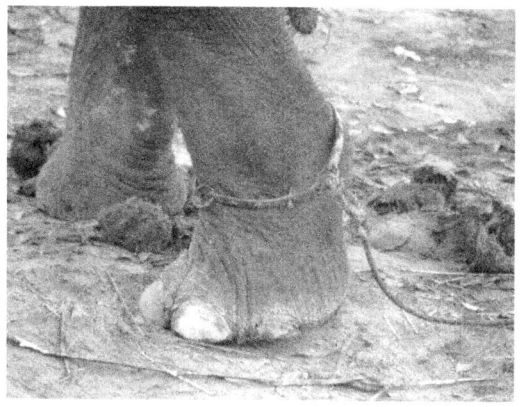

"As a man was passing the elephants, he suddenly stopped, confused by the fact that these huge creatures were being held by only a small rope tied to their front leg. No chains, no cages. It was obvious that the elephants could, at anytime, break away from their bonds. But for some reason, they did not.

He saw a trainer nearby and asked why these animals just stood there and made no attempt to get away.

"Well," the trainer said, "when they are very young and much smaller, we use the same size rope to tie them and, at that age, it's enough to hold them. As they grow up, they are conditioned to believe they cannot break away. They believe the rope can still hold them, so they never try to break free."

The man was amazed. These animals could at any time break free from their bonds. But because they believed they couldn't, they were stuck right where they were.

Like the elephants, how many of us go through life hanging onto a belief that we cannot do something, simply because we failed at it once before?

"Failure is part of learning; we should never give up the struggle in life".

~ **AUTHOR UNKNOWN**

If we really look at what is tying us down, we will see that it is a breakable rope. We don't have to be the product of our environment. Sometimes, just like the elephant, we don't think we are strong enough because we are conditioned from day one to think that we can't do it—that we don't have the strength.

Hopefully, from what I shared with you in this book, you can recognize that you do have the strength. You have the courage to stand tall.

Like my dad told me many years ago, "You can do anything, as long as you put your mind to it."

Wilfred A. Peterson said:
"Walk with the dreamers, the believers, the courageous, the cheerful, the planners, the doers, the successful people with their heads in the clouds and their feet on the ground. Let their spirit ignite a fire within you to leave this world better than when you found it..."

In order for us to move forward, we need to have the courage to walk away, discover the courage to fight, find the courage to be different, seek the courage to let others in, treasure the courage to speak, reach for the courage to change, value the courage to trust, realize the courage to stay, seize the courage to jump, and forever and in all ways, embody the Courage to Stand Tall.

"Sometimes all you need is twenty seconds of insane **COURAGE** *and I promise you something great will come out of it."*

~ BENJAMIN MEE FROM WE BOUGHT A ZOO

BOOK DONNEY TO SPEAK

If you know a group or organization that would benefit from this message at a future event.

Contact Donney for speaking opportunities:
EMAIL: donney@courage2shift.com
WEBSITE: www.donneysalazar.com
FACEBOOK: Courage to Stand Tall

COURAGE comes when you have to face your fears head on. Donney knows what courage is all about. He has overcome the affects of an abusive and alcoholic father, and a mother, stepfather and brother who all dealt and abused drugs. His childhood was marred because of his family's involvement with a prison gang in San Jose, CA. Donney has proven he has the courage to stand tall through all the bullying and abuse, even though he stands at 5'2". Donney is a courageous leader who has shifted the direction of his life from the abusive and gang world he grew up in, to one of successful entrepreneurship.

ABOUT
THE AUTHOR

DONNEY KNOWS WHAT COURAGE IS ALL ABOUT.

He has overcome the effects of an abusive and alcoholic father, and a mother, stepfather and brother who all dealt and abused drugs. His childhood was marred because of his family's involvement with a prison gang in San Jose, CA. Donney has proven he has the courage to stand tall through the obstacles and challenges of life, even though he stands at 5'2". Donney is a courageous leader who has shifted the direction of his life from the gangster world he grew up in, to one of successful entrepreneurship.

Donney is a leader who understands the difference between earning and demanding the respect you are shown. Donney is the co-owner of two organizations; DFS Marketing LLC., and Jupiter LLP. Both work with organizations to help leaders shift their thinking, earn the respect of their people, and focus on having the courage to stand tall.

Donney will inspire your organization with stories and examples of courage. He will motivate you with his passion for helping people shift in order to reach their highest potential. Donney is PASSIONATE about working with organizations who invest in people.

Made in the USA
Middletown, DE
27 January 2020